D1549510

THE YORKSHIRE DALES

THE YORKSHIRE DALES

Mark Denton

Introduction by Richard Mabey

FRANCES LINCOLN LIMITED

PUBLISHERS

Frances Lincoln Ltd
Aurum Publishing Group
74–77 White Lion Street
London N1 9PF
www.franceslincoln.com

The Yorkshire Dales
Copyright © Frances Lincoln Limited 2013
Text and photographs copyright © Mark Denton 2013
Introduction copyright © Richard Mabey 2013
First Frances Lincoln edition 2013

British Library Cataloguing-in-Publication data
A catalogue record for this book is available from the British Library.

ISBN: 978-0-7112-3282-2

Printed and bound in China
9 8 7 6 5 4 3 2 1

Page 1 Piercing evening light in January enlivens the stones at Brimham Rocks, Nidderdale.

Pages 2–3 The Cumbrian corner of the Yorkshire Dales National Park is a breathtaking 'undiscovered' landscape of Britain. Here the Howgill Fells are seen from Fir Bank on an afternoon in August.

Pages 4–5 Catching the steam train on Ribblehead Viaduct in good light became an obsession of mine, with many more failures than successes. Asking a landscape photographer to shoot something requiring split-second timing is removing him from the comfort zone.

CONTENTS

INTRODUCTION
SQUEEZING THROUGH THE BEAST-GATE: AN OUTSIDER'S VIEW OF THE DALES

Richard Mabey

I suppose I'd been exploring the Yorkshire Dales for about six years before I heard about the ancient tradition of home knitting. I had been a diffident visitor, all too aware of being a stranger in this vast and intricate landscape. Learning about this unlikely trade suddenly made the place seem more human and accessible – like one of those shafts of sunset light that can turn the solemn limestone cliffs near Chapel-le-Dale a shockingly garish pink.

It had gone on for centuries, apparently. All across the north-western Dales, in long winter evenings or brief spells of calm after hay-making, the fellside families – men and children as well as women – turned into cottage clothmakers. And it wasn't a matter of bodging together rough jackets or woolsacks, but of knitting the fine-spun local wool into filigree stockings for the fashion market. The finished goods were collected up from the family groups by men known as 'stockingers' and carted to Kendal or Kirkby Stephen for transmission to London.

This cottage industry persisted until the middle of the nineteenth century, particularly in Dent, a fiercely independent artisans' village in the western Dales, until machine-weaving consigned it to the museum. Even in those mid-Victorian times it must have been a hard-won, uncissified business: the exquisite work being tricked out in candlelight by cold, hard-skinned, farmers' hands. In some areas, knitting was combined with mining as an off-season alternative to sheep-herding, in what must have been one of the strangest cycles in English rural work.

So I don't think the sense of relief this fragment of Dales history gave me had much to do with glimpsing a gentler side to upland farming. But as a writer I did feel a rather presumptuous sense of camaraderie with those knitters. Both of us, after all, pursued our journeyman trades, hawking jew-jaws crafted out of the raw stuff of the landscape, to largely metropolitan clients. And I fancy the Dales freelancers weren't averse to a neat turn of wool, so to speak, and maybe to working into their designs personal local motifs and jokes (as Dalespeople still do when ornamenting the tops of their walls). The knowledge helped lift some of that intruder's discomfort, too, and made me – an off-comer, a nosey writer and a southern softie to boot – feel less of an oddity.

This kind of guilt pervades all kinds of communication about the countryside. It is rooted in the age-old confrontation between stranger and native, and springs from a scepticism about whether the look and feel of a place, let alone the real pulse of its life, can ever truly be appreciated by an outsider. Can the view from the sidelines sometimes catch things overlooked by the native, or is it always a kind of exploitation (or at worst voyeurism), lacking, by definition almost, heart and real empathy? Here Graham Nobles has at least one great advantage over me: he lives and works amid the Pennine dales and moors, and his lyrical but unsentimental pictures are partly those of the local archivist, a role that has always been understood and valued in these remote communities.

For me the Yorkshire Dales have brought these dilemmas more sharply to the surface than any other place outside my home patch. I love them passionately for their flowers and extraordinary rockscapes. I have been touched sometimes to the point of embarrassment by the Dalespeople's unflagging hospitality and warmth to tourists and outsiders. But mine, I confess, has been a fair-weather, passive affection. I moon about among the meadow flowers in June, up to my waist in cranesbills, picking up odd and interesting pebbles, and admiring from afar the network of stone walls that locals have ripped their hands creating for the best part of 2,000 years.

Discovering the knitters helped begin the process of defusing the guilt. But the real turning point came when, in my terms at least, I did some real work in the Yorkshire Dales. One summer some years ago – a summer which included the wettest, coldest June in recent memory – I was involved in making a film about the local landscape, its geology, history and botany. We lived on site during those weeks and were surprised at what a complex relationship documentary film-making can enable you to build up with a place, even in a short time. In countryside like the Dales it comes close to being a kind of rural craft in its own right, needing a close knowledge of local resources, a touch of serendipity, a willingness to defer to the weather and to snatch odd harvests in chaotic order whenever the opportunity arose. Yet film-making is also a kind of tourism, an intrusion into another culture and implicitly an invitation to others to come and gaze in much larger numbers.

The crew and I lived out this odd, bipartisan relationship with the landscape throughout those weeks, usually in pretty close physical contact with it. We were in the odd position of simultaneously working in the landscape, and looking at it as a prospect, and in the end I think we all gained a better understanding of the tangled roles of locals and visitors, workers and holidaymakers in a National Park, and of the storytellers and picture-makers who aspire to arbitrate between them.

The film, *White Rock, Black Water*, was based around the two great elements of the Dales: limestone and the water that has shaped it for millennia. W.H. Auden's poem, 'In Praise of Limestone', proved to be a great influence. In it, Auden sees limestone country as hedonistic, present-oriented, benign and pliable, in contrast to the cryptic and uncompromising wastes of granite, ocean and jungle. And it has these qualities chiefly:

> Because it dissolves in water. Mark these rounded slopes
> With their surface fragrance of thyme and, beneath,
> A secret system of caves and conduits; hear these springs
> That spurt everywhere with a chuckle,
> Each filling a private pool for its fish and carving
> Its own little ravine whose cliffs entertain
> The butterfly and the lizard; examine this region
> Of short distances and definite places:
> What could be more like Mother or a fitter background
> For her son, the flirtatious male who lounges
> Against a rock in the sunlight . . .

A blazing sun in summer constricts the pupils in Wensleydale, near Bainbridge.

Discovering limestone for myself was something that happened in parallel with discovering the northern Dales, and it was a cautious, occasional affair. Up until my early twenties, my experience of Britain's uplands had been based on holidays in the moorlands of Scotland and Wales: sour, granitey places whose character seemed petrified, literally, by their ancient, inscrutable rocks. I used to end up pining for the arable fields and copses of my home in the south, which at least had more blatant signs of the movement and cycles of the seasons.

Then, on walking expeditions with friends, I began to discover the flora of limestone country. In Derbyshire, there were wild columbines, blue and white. On the massive, flat, tabular blocks of Gait Barrows in Lancashire, we saw bloody cranesbill, and found wild strawberries ready stewed by the warmth reflected from the white stones. On honey-coloured pastures at the top of Shap Fell we discovered, almost by divination, our first bird's-eye primroses, whose coral-pink flowers and white-dusted leaves seemed to have been made out of the same stuff as the rock underneath.

Then in the early 1980s, we made it to the Yorkshire Dales themselves. My companion and I had a base in Grassington, on the south-eastern edge of Wharfedale, and the day we arrived, we climbed the river valley, through rough, flowerless pastures alongside a stolid stretch of the Wharfe, where it wouldn't have seemed out of place to play Poohsticks. Then – and it seemed to happen quite suddenly – the limestone broke cover. Pale terraces jutted into the current and made the water froth and dash. Dippers bobbed on boulders worn smooth by countless winter floodraces. The cracks between the rocks were filled with flowers whose colours looked quite piercing against the white stone: veins of purple thyme, tufts of lemon rock-rose. Everything seemed sharper – the sounds of the river, the keening of the curlew, even the air itself.

That afternoon we left the river bank and climbed east up the slow incline towards Conistone Old Pasture, between sheets of rock-rose and mountain pansy. Up at the top we could just glimpse the edge of an aboriginal limestone landscape, a vast boneyard of frost-shattered boulders and sills that wound jaggedly along the contour lines. But between us and the summit was something altogether different, and a reminder of how intimately humans and rock have worked together to shape the surface of the Dales. Ranged all the way up the hill were echelons of stone walls unlike any I had seen before. They were over six feet tall, straight, orderly, sometimes so close that they gave the impression of a complex walled garden, and unnervingly narrow. The stepping stones that had been set in them were as sharp as arrowheads, and climbing over the top was like edging on to the saddle of a racing bicycle. The whole assault course went on up the fellside to nearly 1,000 feet.

It turned out that we were clambering over one of the most intriguing relics of Wharfedale history. The whole of this pasture (like much of the Dales' high ground) was once common grazing, with the 'stint' or proportion allotted to each grazier based on the size of the holdings attached to his or her cottage, and measured by an arcane unit called a 'beast-gate' (one beast-gate was feeding and grazing for one full-grown beast). The problem was that beast-gates were inherited, and repeatedly divided up and sold, and by the end of the eighteenth century disorganised over-grazing was becoming a threat to everyone's livelihood. So in 1801 Conistone applied successfully to Parliament for an Act of Enclosure, and the inhabitants set about dividing up the old common pasture into enclosures that reflected their respective portions of the overall beast-gates. The walls and the labyrinth of small fields they enclosed remain, and everything about them – their texture, the shades of the rocks, even their height (they had to keep in oxen in those days as well as sheep) – reflects the quirky individuality of the landscapes and communities of the different Dales. And I like that ancient, if redundant, notion of the 'beast-gate', the admission ticket to the nourishing delights of the high fells, that seemed like a metaphor for what all us off-comers were hoping to earn.

Another year, a friend and I worked out a long circular tramp, starting at Arncliffe, winding round the south of Malham Tarn, and turning home again along a sunken beck by way of Yew Cogar Scar. We followed stark Nordic names, past Hawkswick and Kilnsey Moor and Clowder, before we slithered down towards the thin beck (which eventually joined the Wharfe), not quite knowing what we had let ourselves in for. The stream-side was easy going at first. It followed a shallow ravine over a wide pebble-bed, and every minute or so clamorous wading birds got up in front of us – common sand-pipers, redshanks, oyster-catchers. We felt a little shamefaced, like blundering schoolboy nesters, but fortunately the birds soon wheeled round to continue whatever they had been up to. Then the beck narrowed, the walls of the ravine towered higher and became thickly tangled with ash and hazel scrub. We had to edge our way past rapids and meanders, and boggy islets tufted with bird's-eye primrose. At one point we found ourselves at the bottom of an immense cascade of tufa, like a petrified waterfall, which ended in an enchanted, glassy pool that seemed as still as the rock itself. A couple of months deeper into summer, and we would have been in it in a trice.

A mile further on we could only move forward by doing a traverse on a four-inch wide ledger under an overhand of ancient yews. We began to feel like real explorers, trekking up some lost gorge – though, to tell the truth, the ledge was only three feet above the beck's surface, and we got back to Arncliffe in time for tea. And in time, too, to escape a dramatic change in

Three lone trees on Twistleton Scar, Ingleton, provide symmetry for a shot over the valley of the River Doe. The possibilities for good compositions up here are almost endless.

the weather. Tongues of cloud were unrolling down the hills to the west, probing the valley and then creeping up the slopes on the other side, like vaporous lava streams. Water refracts the landscape here in all manner of subtle ways.

The whole character of limestone country is shaped by the fundamental, symbiotic relationship that exists between stone and water. Limestone is the supremely weatherable rock. It can be fractured by frost, polished by ice and torrent, dissolved by rain and then be reborn – as tufa or stalactites, say – when the calcium carbonate is re-deposited from solution. It was from water, too, that limestone was created in the first place, built up like a snowdrift from the falling skeletons of countless small sea creatures. Three hundred million years ago, the ancient slates that covered much of the north of Britain lay under warm, shallow seas, brimming with life. There were miniature shrimps, ammonites, molluscs, all lending their calcareous shells to the infinitesimally slow building of the limestone layers. But in the Pennines, and especially over the area that was to become the Yorkshire Dales, there were coral reefs in the warm lagoons, too, full of crinoids, delicately beautiful organisms which look like half starfish, half sea lilies,

rooted on calcite stems and feeding on minute plankton (some of which had shells themselves, like the rosettes of microscopic flowers). Over millions of years the seas rose, filled up with reefs, dried out, returned – but this time, perhaps, with water which was cooler or more silted, and in which mud or sand might be laid down along with the limestone. And as these periods alternated, so the strata that are so characteristic of the limestone scars and terraces of the Dales, ranging from pure white to dirty brown, built up, one on top of the other.

Limestone is at the heart of the Dales. The more I saw of it the more I felt Auden was right, and that it shapes patterns of life and character, as well as the physical landscape. It is warm, adaptable, ingenuous. It wears its history on its sleeve, or like the lines on a human face. It casts a spell which is very different from those usually attributed to conventional 'heritage' landscapes, those 'timeless, immemorial' places where living things have begun to be regarded as inanimate fossils. Limestone – which is exactly this – seems paradoxically to be a rock that has had life breathed back into it.

But I certainly didn't understand how it worked this magic, or indeed many of the more mundane puzzles set by its formations in the Dales. If it was so sensitive to water, for instance, why hadn't it all dissolved away? And, as part of the Pennines, the English uplands, why did it form so few mountainous peaks? Making the film was, in part, an attempt to try and find answers to some of these questions.

We began, in one of the rare moments when the weather let us tell the story in logical order, by climbing from the bottom of the Dales to the very top. On a hot and sparkling day in late May we toiled up Ingleborough, the great sugar-loaf hill that dominates every view in the western Dales, and which the locals call simply 'The Hill' as if there were no other worth a mention. Our idea was to film a panorama of the landscape below from 2,500 feet up. We followed one of Alfred Wainwright's wonderfully illustrated routes, past cairns and pot-holes and ladder-stiles. But with hundredweights of camera gear to haul, it took us all morning, and we were grateful for the occasional breather to pick up shots of the coralline patterns in the rocks, and of the way they cracked and weathered. We began to recognise the motifs that you see repeated time and again in limestone country: glacial scratch marks, shallow circular depressions, runnels, bevel-edged blocks, V-shaped clefts. For their part the stones responded by tripping us up and doing their own non-too-delicate etching on our hands – a salutary reminder that the calcium carbonate in limestone is also one of the raw materials of human bones.

When we reached the hard, millstone-grit plateau that caps Ingleborough, we could see almost the whole of the Dales landscape stretched out below, and there was an unmistakeable pattern to it. The river valleys, the true Dales, carry hay meadows on their richer soils. Higher up the fellside are the enclosed pastures, and above them the common grazing, the drifts of scree and the flat limestone pavements lying below terraces of limestone. Many of the valleys seem carved in a wide and gentle U-shape, a legacy of the glaciers of the last Ice Age. They rasped their way across the Dales 20,000 years ago, rounding off the profiles of hills and widening the embryo river valleys, scouring the limestone bare in some places and dumping drifts of gravel and clay in others.

We were reaping the rewards of our five-hour climb with sweeping pans over this airy mosaic, when we had a reminder of just what a varied playground the Dales National Park had become. Over the far rim of the summit appeared the toiling body of a London student on a mountain bike. He had cycled up the mountain, by a steeper route than ours, in something under 30 minutes. We slipped him a five pound note and filmed him careering about the crags – one of the shapes, maybe, of climbing to come. Then we all had a go.

One puzzle stood out above all others from this eagle eye's view. For a landscape so famously shaped by and inextricably entwined with water – where was it all? All we could see were a couple of the bigger rivers and flashes of sunlight from the thinner streams, most of which seemed to vanish down holes. And that, it turned out, was the answer. Most of the water is underground, seeping down through swallow-holes, pot-holes, cracks in rocks, leaking river beds. The Dales are constantly being eaten away by water trying to reach an even lower level. In some places you can put your ear to the rock and hear it, the deceptively comforting murmur of water wearing away the stone.

The next day we followed it, down into Weathercote Cave – one of the most extraordinary of the underground chambers which catacomb the Dales. There is a waterfall inside it, lit up by the sun where part of the cave roof has collapsed. No wonder Turner was entranced by it during his painting tours of the Dales in the early 1800s. He first visited Weathercote

The hidden gem of Mill Gill Force waterfall, near the *All Creatures Great and Small* village of Askrigg.

in 1808, and made the perilous 70-foot descent to the bottom just to see the marvel of a cascade of water falling out of the sunlight. On his second trip, though, in 1816, he couldn't even get into the cave. The rain had been so heavy for weeks that the underground rivers were in spate and the cave was half-full of water. Turner had to make do with a rapid sketch from the top, noting in his sketch book 'entrance impassable'. (In Yordas Cave, a couple of miles to the west, his problem was darkness, not water. He had to sketch without seeing what he was drawing, and scrawled labels and annotations all over the page: 'loose stones'; 'day light'; 'roof'.) Did he glimpse one of Weathercote's ethereal rainbows on his first visit? He put one in his finished picture, painted in 1809, arching mistily above his own figure, which he included in the picture at the bottom of the cave, bowed over a sketch pad on a boulder.

The tumbling water still fills the cavern with an eerie, almost luminous mist and we see rainbows in the spray, too. It is cold and slippery inside, and I edge gingerly into a position beside a huge fallen block of limestone known as Mahomet's Coffin, which hangs suspended between roof and floor. Suddenly, as I lean forward, one of the rainbows flips over on its side and forms a circle, completely surrounding me at chest level, like a fallen halo. And above us, joining sky to earth in yet another way, spotted flycatchers are swooping into the cave and catching midges in the sunbeams.

But not all the landscape here is in tidy historical layers. That afternoon we went up to Norber, above the village of Austwick, where a spectacular range of brooding sandstone boulders – 'erratics' from another place and another geological era – were dumped on top of the limestone some time during the last Ice Age. It is humbling evidence of the power of the glaciers that these deadweight boulders were scattered like so many dice hundreds of feet from their original beds. Some of them eventually found a role as landmarks. The very first walls here, built in the Iron Age, were made out of stones cleared from the fields, and would have had to follow – and include – anything as immovable as the Norber giants. So they survive as corner-stones in some of the oldest surviving walls in the country. Others perch on eroded limestone plinths like the wreckage of a megalithic temple.

We film under them, over them, through them – picking up atmospherically framed shots of early purple orchids, sleeping sheep and views which stretch as far as the Lancashire coast. Once we glimpse a peregrine falcon careering high over Moughton Fell to the north. But we also encounter a problem that was to dog us more and more over the succeeding days. We grapple for shots of flowers growing in cracks in the rock, and ferns curling round impossible corners, our efforts symbolising a deeper dilemma that we never entirely resolve: in a landscape which is so fantastically and richly variegated, what is the representative shot, the 'right view'? Who chooses, and how?

But on that halcyon evening, up in the exhilarating air of Norber, such philosophical hair-splitting is a long way from our minds. We finish work by sunset and set off down the hill, looking forward to drinks in Austwick as the swifts scream round the stone cottages. I volunteer to take the first shift carrying the camera, and am in too high-spirited a mood to pay respectful attention to the terrain. Halfway down the hill I lose my footing on a wet rock, and start to fall away. But some perverse instinct makes me think of the camera's safety more than my own. I stretch out to try and keep my balance, and feel, in awful slow motion (I am almost sure I hear it, too) the muscle in the front of my right thigh tearing.

For the next few days I have to stay in long shot and not move around too much for fear of falling over again, or, heaven forbid, ruining continuity. My fatuous notion that I might be shown helping out in a drystone-walling sequence, scripted to show the next stage in the evolution of the Dales drystone wall network, is thankfully knocked on the head by the fact that I have to be a hundred yards away, peering at the scene like a passing hiker. Two boys from a local farm do the job brilliantly, and are quite happy to knock down a perfectly good wall just to build it up again for the camera.

Instead I am sent up in a helicopter, for aerial views of the walls and limestone pavements. I argue passionately against such technological intrusion into what has so far been a fairly grass-roots, organic filming style; but really it is terror speaking, not editorial judgement. My nerves aren't improved by a sad accident near the helicopter landing pad: a female swallow is lying dead on the grass after flying full tilt into the plate-glass window of the car showroom next door. Her mate is flying back and forth and settling uncomprehendingly by her body.

But it isn't a bad omen, and not my day to be added to the scree. The flight is short and steady, and the views are awesome. From 1,000 feet up the whole limestone plateau appears like a dazzling white engraving that stretches from horizon to horizon. The patterns of holes and cracks and walls – dividing, joining, widening – remind me of nothing so much as the intricate network of creeks in a Norfolk saltmarsh. It is that black, remorseless water again. . . . When we land, the male swallow is still in a state of distress and is trying to mount his dead mate. I can't bear it any longer and bury her away in the corner of the meadow.

This is uncompromisingly hard country. The roads are littered with the corpses of birds and sheep. We heard of two tragic accidents in our first week, and saw the results of another. A pot-holer had fallen into the blackness of Gaping Gill, and a child had drowned in a ravine near Thornton Force waterfall. And one night, as were driving along a switchback road to

Settle for supper, we passed the spot where a hiker had been hit by a car not long before. Her backpack and dead Yorkshire terrier were still lying by the side of the road, a terrible, chilling sight. We were all shocked, and made our own resolves not to sanitise this place.

The next part of the story took us, ironically, to the Thornton Force ravines near Ingleton, where the child had drowned. After the upheavals of ancient earth movements and glaciers, woodland began to invade the Dales about 8,000 years ago. Most of it has long been cleared to make way for grazing, but around the dramatic series of twisting ravines known as the Ingleton Falls, a combination of ancient, infertile rocks and intractable topography combined to preserve some of the woodland intact. But there was an additional reason for this local survival. A century earlier, this patch of picturesque scenery had become one of Britain's first 'nature' reserves – and certainly the first to be run as a commercial concern. In 1885, aware of the growing appeal of hill walking to the workers in nearby cities, an enterprising local man called Joseph Carr proposed that Ingleton village should open up its beauty spots, and, in effect, market its scenery. He predicted that 'When our trades people shall provide better accommodation and the natural beauties of the neighbourhood are laid open to the public . . . people from far and near will resort to Ingleton for the salubrity of its air and the geological wonders that abound on every hand.' So access was negotiated with local landowners, bridges and walkways were built, and what came to be called 'The Ingleton Scenery Company' opened for business on Good Friday, 1885. At Whitsun, so many people came on special trains that the village ran out of food, and had to take the unprecedented step of baking bread on a Sunday.

Joseph Carr's venture was an early model for the modern rural tourist industry, but it had the additional side effect of conserving the tree cover in the steep ravines and around the falls, so that it is still possible to see something of what the Dales woodlands must once have been like. Much of it, because of locally acidic rocks, is old oak coppice. But there is ashwood, too, on more alkaline soils, of the kind that must have once covered most of the hills. In these humid river gorges the trees grow very tall, and the dappled, rippling pattern of shade they cast adds to the impression that everything here is shaped or touched by water. We filmed a wood-warbler singing its shivering, liquid song, and the sapphire glow of wood forget-me-nots in the damp hollows. With my leg still stiff I was finding it hard to balance on the wet, streamside rocks. I padded around, sitting down whenever I could. And on one of these enforced rests, peering nervously into the water, I spotted a pebble trapped in a hole in the river-bed limestone, whirling endlessly in the current. Its impact was imperceptible. But in a few hundred years it would have ground out a crater. This shape, worn out in fathomless

pot-holes and tiny circular dents, gouged out of the floors of caves and a favourite ornament for cottage walls, is stamped across limestone country like a signature.

We had a treat at lunchtime, a couple of bottles of white wine cooled in the stream. But it was hard to relax. The danger – a nagging shadow of slithery rock and dark water – seemed never very far away.

That was the last full filming day we had. For the next three days – the first in 'flaming June' – we could barely shoot at all through the gales and rain, save for long views of Ingleborough and the patterns of terracing in the valleys. Even these shots were hard work in the unrelentingly cold north winds. When we tried to capture the great U-shaped Dale, it took four of us to hold the camera tripod steady. We were repeatedly driven back to the shelter of the cars, and marvelled at the lapwing chicks, newly hatched in the pastures and seemingly oblivious to the cold.

But one torrential overnight storm did provide us with a bonus. These downpours, rushing off the hills, can top up the underground rivers and cave systems in a matter of hours, and I have seen the overflows come gushing like fountains out of bare hillsides. There was nothing quite as dramatic as this the morning after the storm, but we did find a dried out beck now in full spate just below Norber. We followed it down the hill, and saw it already forming miniature waterfalls and wallows – forking, taking short cuts, washing pebbles down the hill, and forming new lime-rich flushes around the patches of bird's-eye primrose and butterwort. At Thornton Force there was a tideline of debris and leaf-litter twenty feet above the usual level of the river.

After a few days the weather settled a little. It was good to have the chance to see the place in a more restful mood. I wandered up towards Moughton Fell, a high plateau of shattered stones and clattering slabs that stretches from the eastern foot of Ingleborough as far as the River Ribble. It is a landscape pared down to the bone. All that remains of a great juniper wood that once grew here are a few stumps bleached to the same colour as the rock. Yet even here there is evidence of the human compulsion to leave a mark on the landscape. There are cairns scattered everywhere, some no more than little shark-fin stones raised on their edges and wedged in a crack. They are, I suppose, just signatures, marks to say someone was here in this lonely place.

I dropped down to a beck that flows out of the Ribble, a warmer and friendlier spot, and began to amble about more slowly. Out of the corner of my eye I spotted a bundle of feathers. It was a fresh peregrine kill, a racing pigeon with its identification ring still incongruously bright among the bloody feathers. I sat and pondered that unsettling number, and its evidence of the individuality of life. The whole Dales landscape is like that really: specific and idiosyncratic, a region, as Auden had written, 'of short distances and definite places'. Sitting still for once I began to notice small clumps of bird's-eye primroses (the flower of the Dales) growing on islands in the beck, out of the way of nibbling sheep, and, in the drystone wall I was leaning against, layers of an exquisitely striped rock called banded whetstone. Wading into the stream I found more of it, and had an absurd but oddly pleasant fantasy of becoming a prospector.

But that evening we were back at work. We needed to explore more of what happened to limestone underground, and were booked to spend the night in Ingleborough cave. This vast and labyrinthine cavern is the drainage channel for much of the water caught by The Hill. But now it is also a show cave, which is why we had to film by night. Before we arrived the interior had been lit by a team of electricians who trundled their gear around the cave in wheelbarrows. For their benefit as much as anything, we began at the far end of the cave and worked our way backwards.

The tunnels are rough and narrow beyond the public areas, and I had to crawl through them on all fours, using a torch to try and pick out for the camera the scratches made when the glacial melt-waters hurtled debris through this cave at more than 100 miles per hour. But I could hardly complain. When the first Victorian cavers broke into these chambers, they were often up to their chests in water, and, in the words of one of them, used their 'stomachs as sledges, and mouths as candleholders'.

Ingleborough Cave is full of extraordinary limestone sculpture. The rainwater that drains into the cavern dissolves limestone on its way down, and when it emerges into the air in the underground chambers a little of the water evaporates and leaves behind a minute new crystal of calcium carbonate. The profusion and variety of rock forms here is amazing and baffling – not just conventional stalactites and stalagmites, but stalks that curl sideways out of the cave wall, like pigs' tails. One group of these has clustered like pipecleaners. Another has grown with enough tension to ring like a tuning fork when it is struck. And there are bigger masses of tufa, too, shaped like vast sides of meat, or draped curtains. Occasionally the water seeping into the cave is so over-rich with calcium that the crystals settle out as 'cave coral' – a reminder of the real coral that created limestone, and that the slowly growing architecture of these caves is a precise allegory of how the whole landscape works: water turning to rock, the rock slowly leaching into water, then returning to rock again. In the end the whole cave will go through this cycle, because coral and tufa, stalactite and stalagmite, will go on growing until they have filled every inch of space. Then there will be darkness again here, for the ringing rocks, the glittering cave coral, even the albino shrimps that have somehow adapted to this environment. When we had first come here to reconnoitre the location on an ordinary public tour, our guide had turned off the lights for exactly 60 seconds, to give us a taste of total darkness, and the director, Caroline, and I had grasped each other instinctively like terrified medievals. Ever since, I have found myself pondering, and failing to grasp, the conundrum of those fabulous forms and colours locked up in unexplored caves – and locked inside other rocks, for that matter, never to see the light or be seen.

But above the cave, like a mirror image of the roof, the limestone

Bolton Castle stands proud on the slopes of Wensleydale, on a summer afternoon of heavy, bubbling clouds.

pavements are perennially sparkling. They are the most remarkable natural monuments in the Dales, tables of the hardest limestone which were scraped clean of soil by the glaciers, cracked by earth movements, and eaten away along their fault lines by rainwater. The cracks, known as 'grykes', are full of flowers – as are the depressions and hummocks on the 'clints', the slabs of rock between.

We had made repeated attempts to film on a pavement, but were either beaten back by the lack of light, or the limitations of our equipment. There was still that problem of how and what to film. The surfaces and vegetation of the pavement are so rich and intricate (and treacherous) that we had to mark our routes, plant discoveries and possible vantage points for the camera with ribbon-decked bamboo poles. And the underlying aesthetic dilemma, of just how to present this panoply of riches, remained, and forced each of us to consider what the place meant to us. I fancied, without having thought of the complications this would present for the rest of the team, doing the whole sequence as a piece of unrehearsed cinéma-vérité, leaping from plant to plant, and hoping that the sense of spontaneous discovery would make its own point about the natural diversity of the place. The director, understandably, wanted a sense of direction and for me to justify the relevance of what I was doing. Richard, the cameraman, needed to know where I was going to move next – and to be able to make the best use of his specialised equipment in revealing the detail of rock and plant.

I felt then (and do even more now) that these different perspectives were a kind of metaphor for the differing views of the multitude of people who use the Dales; so it was fortunate that a compromise worked itself out, in which we were all able to put across most of what we wanted to say. We worked for two full days, whenever there was enough sunlight, on a patch of pavement no more than 600 feet square, and could easily have gone on for a week. I have in front of me the stack of snapshots I took on those two days. They seem, with hindsight, to tell two intertwined stories: one of the marvellous exploitation of this intricate habitat by the limestone flora; the other of the more awkward adaptation by a group of humans trying to find their own feet in it.

There is the camera's first tentative descent into a gryke – but what a gryke: it is grooved and fluted on both sides like an elaborate Gothic cloister. There is a portrait of Caroline posed behind an immense bouquet of ferns which have grouped themselves quite naturally in a bowl in the rock. There are snaps of other pits and grooves and crevices: a clump of butter-yellow globe-flowers snuggling in a kind of limestone settle; tadpole runnels, the first tear-shaped breaches that water makes in the surface of the rock, which will gradually push forward their tapered ends until they meet a fully-fledged gryke; Richard's head poking above a gryke that seems no more than a foot wide, and which runs almost dead straight towards the brow of Ingleborough in the background.

Then he is four feet below the surface, his shoulders wedged between the walls of the gryke, filming ferns and wild garlic blooms which have been drawn up three feet tall towards the light. The grykes, providing all the humidity and shade of woods, are full of woodland plants – early purple orchid, herb paris, rivers of bluebells and solitary primroses. But they have

A beautifully crafted 'water staircase' at West Burton Falls in Bishopdale.

trees, too – hazel, holly, buckthorn, bird cherry – some barely reaching above ground level, others winding horizontally along the lips of the grykes. There is an ancient ash, pruned by wind and browsing animals to the shape of an almost perfect hemisphere. A sheet of flowering lilies-of-the-valley so dense that they completely cover the rock. And then there are the pictures of us, lounging about as we eat our lunchtime picnic, looking as if we were having an easier time than we were.

But the limestone has not had an easy time itself. In 1951, over one thousand tons of Ingleborough limestone were grubbed out to create, ironically, an exhibit for the Festival of Britain on 'The Origins of the Land.' It's doubtful if that could happen now. The Wildlife and Countryside Act of 1981 created the opportunity in law of making Limestone Pavement Orders (LPOs). Any limestone pavement can be notified by a local authority, and removal of rock from the designated site by commercial quarries (and, strictly speaking, by acquisitive householders too) then becomes a criminal offence. All the remaining limestone pavements in the Dales are now protected by LPOs imposed by the National Park Authority.

But in the 1980s, quarrying, chiefly for rough quality material for the chemical industry, was still in full sway. On one filming day we witnessed the macabre spectacle of a slab of pavement which had been dug up and dumped with all its flowers still in bloom – except that they were now having to grow upside down.

But the quarrying issue is not as clear cut as this. Limestone is a valuable raw material, and digging it has been a livelihood in the Dales for centuries. The poet Norman Nicholson, who lived in the limestone country of Cumbria, to the west, saw small-scale mining and quarrying as essentially rural industries, like the harvesting of root-crops. There has always been a tradition of stone gathering too, and not just for drystone walls. Throughout the Dales you will still see roofs and walls ornamented with limestone gargoyles and natural sculptury, 'found stones' in the shapes of rabbits, cockerels, Yorkshire terriers, that have simply been picked up on the hills. This is a very local, vernacular craft, not much more harmful than gathering windfalls.

The acceptability of quarrying is a matter of scale and place. A National Park ought perhaps to have a small National Quarry, to celebrate the role raw rock has played in the region's economic history. The place for quarrying should be precisely where the features are not on the surface but hidden, unshaped, underground, where excavation could then create new exposed limestone landscapes, rather than obliterate existing ones.

The kind of instinct that tempts walkers to create cairns and farmers to decorate their barns with limestone hares may give clues as to the way the Dales is likely to develop in the future. It is – again Auden was prophetically

right – a very festive landscape. If its role as a productive farming area is declining, so its other identity – first formally recognised when the Ingleton Scenery Company was created, but going back, I would bet, much further – is being relished by residents and visitors alike. Barns that once stored hay are being converted into cheap stopovers for long-distance walkers. The remaining old hay-meadows, anachronisms in hard-bitten economic terms, are cherished not just as reserves for wild flowers, but as quality food sources for the specialised dairy herds (goats included) that are helping in the renaissance of local British cheeses. Farmers on Japanese four-wheeled motorcycles herd sheep, while hang-gliders wheel overhead. The Yorkshire Dales is a place where you can play without feeling foolish, make your own personal engagements with the elements of rock, water and wind. And it has this quality, I believe, because nature has been a more or less equal partner in the evolution of the landscape, not whipped into submission as it has been across so much of England. Yet it has never spurned people. Their history is etched in the limestone, and you would be hard put to find a better model of reconciliation between town and country.

And it would have been difficult to find a happier symbol of this whole process than the event we were lucky enough to film for our closing sequence. It was at Hardraw Force near Hawes, the highest unbroken waterfall in England. Hardraw tumbles into a kind of natural amphitheatre, where it is possible, as Wordsworth discovered, to scramble behind the falls and stand under the overhang: 'We found the rock, which before had appeared like a wall, extending itself over our heads like the ceiling of a huge cave, from the summit of which the water shot directly over our heads into a basin, and among fragments wrinkled over with masses of ice as white as snow, or rather, as Dorothy says, like congealed froth. The water fell at least two yards from us, as we stood directly behind it . . .' [letter to Coleridge, 1799]. In the severe winter of 1739, the falls became a column of ice, solid enough, save for a thin current of water through the core, for the local people to dance around.

What we found two and a half centuries later was a summer festival in the same spirit – a brass band concert that is held most years in the natural 'basin' at the foot of Hardraw, with its extraordinary acoustics. So it was that our film ended, very fittingly, with the sound of Vaughan Williams vying with the roar of water and the clamour of the jackdaws that nest on the cliffs around the falls. It was a gala day for the local people, and a kind of Harvest Home for us.

SWALEDALE
AND THE NORTH

A single stone barn near Muker, on an early summer afternoon of shifting dramatic light. There are few places in the world this could be other than the Yorkshire Dales.

Pages 16–17 The barns of upper Swaledale in snow. One of the most iconic views of the Dales and also one of my favourites.

It's difficult to avoid photographing sheep in the Dales, so you may as well make a feature of them. On the left a small flock graze at Oxnop in summer, a beautifully formed little valley to the south of Swaledale. On the right a spring lamb waits momentarily in front of the undulating drystone wall near Reeth.

The 'rollercoaster' wall near Reeth in front of Fremington Edge is one of my favourite 'micro-landscapes' of the Dales, though I'm sure there are many more I have so far missed. The early leaves might give a false impression of this being autumn, but the white blossom of the hawthorn trees correctly dates this as late spring. Only a stray telegraph wire interrupts the scene.

A classic view of Gunnerside in late spring. The colours are so much more vibrant at this time of year than later in the summer as the grass turns a darker green and leaves more leathery. A scattering of wildflowers, for which Swaledale is famous, break up the foreground.

Wain Wath Falls are a series of gentle waterfalls on the upper reaches of the River Swale. Here the river cuts through yellow limestone and forms fascinating shapes in the rock. Shooting into the sun is unusual for me in these circumstances, but taming the sun behind tree branches makes it possible.

Three great valleys of the Dales, Wensleydale, Garsdale and Mallerstang, all begin from the high point of Garsdale Head. To the north runs Mallerstang and the upper reaches of the River Eden. The small ruin of Pendragon Castle is found here. One of the tallest peaks of the Dales, Wild Boar Fell is seen to the south-west from here, on a sunny but bitterly cold winter day.

MALHAM
AND THE SOUTH

Running water is very common is the Dales, standing water much less so thanks to the porous nature of the limestone here. In the southern Dales it's a little more common. Above a spectacular sunset is reflected in the largest natural lake of the Dales, Malham Tarn. Below, a windy day at Kilnsey Crag, though the small fishing lakes to the south of the village remain still enough to provide reflections, being protected by the Wharfedale valley cliffs.

Pages 32–33 There are many small, but spectacular waterfalls in the Dales. This wall of water belongs to Scala Force near Hebden, in Wharfedale.

Waterfalls in the southern Dales are often tucked away in gullies that would be easily missed by walkers were it not for local knowledge. This is the stunning Catrigg Force near Stainforth. At the time of writing the waterfall and surrounding dell are up for sale, with ideas of converting it into a mini hydro-electric scheme. I trust it's an estate agent's fantasy that would never get past the planners!

Pages 36–37 The view across Ribblesdale from Winskill Stones fascinated me for months while shooting this book, particularly at the spot where it is framed by a twisted tree that seems to grow out of solid rock. It was difficult to get around on the tops in a two-wheel-drive car, but just about possible, with a few helping hands to push me out of trouble at one point. I missed a few good opportunities to shoot at this precise spot I suspect, but caught this bleak scene in January, enlivened above by splitting cloud formations.

A windy summer morning near Thorpe in Wharfedale.
The valley flattens out here as you look towards the small
town of Grassington, and I use the windblown grass to add
foreground interest. Weather in the Dales is rarely boring,
unless the rain really sets in!

Pages 40–41 One of the classic views of the Dales, from the limestone karst on top of Malham Cove, looking south over the short expanse of Malhamdale and further afield to the hills of Lancashire. The largest peak on the right turns out to be Pendle Hill, something I only discovered after driving aimlessly one day from Skipton when weather conditions were frustrating.

Drystone walls criss-cross the Dales everywhere, including here at the entrance to the spectacular gorge of Gordale Scar. It's the type of landscape feature that might have terrified Victorian townsfolk. While a walk into the jaws is highly recommended I found that better photographs were achieved on the outskirts, and it was easier to give scale to the place by including a man-made feature.

I don't especially like the idea of driving a 4 x 4, so getting around in the Dales after snow is awkward. During this week in January 2012 I was staying in Skipton, from where it is certainly easier to access some roads cutting into the southern hills. The road up from Langcliffe to Halton Gill was mostly clear (farmers often help out) and I was able to catch some fabulous morning cloudscapes and Pen-y-ghent picked out in strong sunlight.

Few places in the Dales or even England seem to glory more in autumnal colour than Bolton Abbey. I crossed the River Wharfe to find a better vantage point having been working next to the Abbey in stronger sunlight. Shooting into the sun is often ruled out, but not so much on a hazy evening like this one. I hid the sun behind tree branches and it still had the strength to cast delicious light into the foreground.

Photographs of rainbows always seem quite impressive to people, for their scarcity. The truth is they're not that scarce at all. Spend time out in showers and broken cloud and sooner or later you'll spot one. The trickier aspect is finding yourself in a location where a rainbow works with the composition. Most of this is pure luck, but the more you try . . . of course. Here a double rainbow hangs over the village of Burnsall on a blustery summer morning.

NIDDERDALE
AND THE EAST

Perspectives on the Dales don't come much more familiar than this even if
you're not aware of the precise location. This is the classic view from the Shawl at
Leyburn (or rather after a good 20 minute walk along the ridge). Finding the right
moment for this shot took patience, and at times I saw better colour on the trees,
but without any interest in the sky. Waiting for another year is often best, and this
is what it took to achieve the shot with conditions that satisfied me.

Three images from the sublime Fountains Abbey and Studley Royal gardens.
I eschewed the popular shot down the waterway this time and found a
tighter angle on the Abbey itself, surrounded by autumn colour (of course
an essential time to visit). A detail shot of one of the weirs reflects more
autumnal highlights, and finally the classic perspective of the Temple of Piety
through the pine trees. I could probably shoot a whole book within
this square mile.

Pages 58–59 After a parched early springtime, 2012 made up for the lack of water by providing it almost constantly for the rest of the year. During a relatively rare break in the clouds I headed out to see what the excess rainfall was doing to the local waterfalls. The answer at West Burton was racing water, which also made the pulse race. The beck is normally comfortably crossed in wellies, but any closer than this would have spelled danger. Later, in September, our village experienced the highest flooding levels in living memory.

January of 2012 was considerably drier than later in the year, and I approached closer to West Burton falls for a detailed shot of the fascinating ice sculptures formed by melting and refreezing of the water. The winter didn't quite get cold enough to freeze the Wensleydale falls that year, but it had in the previous two bitter years. Visiting Hardraw at this time proved quite an experience with huge icicles dangling way above the falls, and plenty of evidence they were falling off and hitting the path below.

Two views of upper Nidderdale, in different seasons. The first shows the enticing tourist attraction of How Stean Gorge in autumn, where my six-year-old daughter had great fun donning a hard hat and scrambling along the narrow pathways guided by steel ropes. In the second, thousands of wildflowers burst forth in summer on the nature walk at Studfold Farm, another great spot for a family day out.

Summer 2012, and even when the sun broke free it seemed heavy rainfall wasn't far away. Here I'm high up on the moor above Coverdale, looking to Great Whernside in the far distance. Topping the scene a huge anvil thundercloud appears, somehow giving the sense of African savannah. More thunderclouds were visible to the north-east over the Vale of York, and were appearing at a rate of a least one a day during this turbulent spell of weather.

One walk, two views. It's worth walking along the Leyburn Shawl at
any time of year, but autumn and winter pay particular dividends.
As often in winter, the sun struggled to break fully through the clouds,
being so close to the horizon, but that helped me balance the images.
It's never great to have an uninhibited sun beaming straight into the
lens. Shafts of light above Penn Hill warmed the freezing day a touch,
and on the route back the cloud closed in, but allowed an atmospheric
image of a cluster of pine trees, with an alpine feel to it.

A summer evening in Coverdale, and a rare expanse of water appears. Pinker's Pond as it is known comes and goes with the rain, but this summer provided plenty, and I was able to imitate the Lake District by taking a closer angle. The location is popular with courting couples, I'm told, but I didn't see any on this particular evening. Perhaps my lens and the constant buzz of midges put them off.

Turbulent cloud churns over Penn Hill and the cemetery at Leyburn in the foreground. My American agent often says 'What great skies you have over there, Mark', and I guess they are right. The Dales often seem to mix up the cloud from the prevailing weather in the west. I've noticed that lenticular cloudforms are relatively common near Coverdale (beyond Penn Hill in this image). That's good for me, as I think skies are much more crucial in panoramic work than in other formats of landscape photography.

More fine summer skies at Middleham Castle. Middleham is just outside the National Park, but it is most certainly a Dales village, feeling charming and authentic at the same time. Conversation in the pubs often centres around horse racing; there are a number of stables here and a large gallops across the moorland towards Penn Hill.

RIBBLESDALE
AND THE WEST

Pages 74–75 Strange conditions at Ribblehead, with a partial rainbow briefly forming, but only where the sun pierces the cloud. This is Batty Moss, a continual favourite spot of mine over the years. You're in the centre of a huge bowl, with options for shooting in three directions. A veritable theatre of landscape.

Pages 76–77 Dentdale is narrow and dramatic, but my favourite view is from the top, next to the road before it dips below the Denthead Viaduct. I tried a number of times to catch the steam train on top, but it never coincided with the light I demanded for the shot. A tough ask really . . . I suspect I shall keep trying though.

A classic view of the outer Dales, from Fox's Pulpit near Sedburgh. These are the Howgill Fells, and for me the most beautiful little mountain range in England. I half expected a couple of hobbits to scurry past, or maybe the Riders of Rohan. It is quite bizarre that this place is almost ignored, despite being next to a busy motorway and sandwiched between the Lake District and the central Dales.

Another view from the heights of Twistleton Scar. The prevailing
winds here head east from the Irish Sea (Morecambe Bay is
visible from up here), twisting any tree to grow in that direction.
This one looks to have put up quite a brave resistance against the
wind over the years and is now a truly remarkable shape.

Waterfalls are plentiful on the western slopes of the Dales. Left, the River Twiss heads over Thornton Force in autumn, draining from the Whernside and Twistleton area. Below, I'm perched awkwardly above Cautley Spout in the Howgills looking almost directly downwards. Risk taking is not a big hobby of mine, and I'm pleased there's a good ledge of rock before the main drop.

Ingleborough dominates many views in this part of the Dales. It's not the highest peak in the National Park. This distinction belongs to its less recognisable neighbour, Whernside, but it's certainly the most prominent. Above is a classic view from Batty Moss at Ribblehead, on a frozen December morning, and below a much more distant perspective of the Ingleborough range from high up in Langstrothdale to the east.

Pages 84–85 The Howgill range stands proud from any angle. Here the snow-capped peaks are seen from Uldale to the east. There are many great walking routes from here, and the area seems totally unspoilt by tourism, almost undiscovered.

The view from Batty Moss at Ribblehead in the opposite direction, toward the peak of Pen-y-ghent, which from here appears as a mere bump on the horizon. Evening light catches the lumps of limestone and the moon rises behind the peak.

The triple streams of Beezley Falls at Ingleton seem designed for my panoramic camera. It was approaching dusk on the autumn evening when I took this shot, but applying a heavy warm-up filter to correct the colours I simply extended the exposure time to 30 seconds, blurring out the water and discovering mini whirlpools at the bottom of the waterfall.

Pages 92–93 Littondale seems to be the geographic centre of the Dales, and is absolutely magnificent. Not many seem to venture up the road that branches off in Wharfedale near Kilnsey, and they are missing out on a perfect valley, seemingly lost in time. The exciting feature of Cowside Beck cuts through the fields to the west, but before it lies a glorious landscape of drystone walls and barns.

Halfway up Wensleydale lies a small but very noticeable mound called Lady Hill. I spent the best part of two years driving past the curious clump of pine trees, and rarely stopping, because the light or conditions never matched my lofty aims for a shot of the place. Finally in the last months of shooting I drove back from Hawes on a stormy summer evening and caught mountainous thunderclouds behind the hill, and lengthening shadows on the grass before it.

A triptych of valley features from the central Dales. First is the view from Bardale
Head down Raydale and eventually to Semer Water, looking like a small puddle
from here, and Wensleydale beyond. This is the highest point in the Dales easily
accessible by car. On the right is a view at the top of Cowside Beck in Littondale,
looking back towards the place where I shot the image on page 92. Finally, late
summer light cascades into Langstrothdale. This was technically a tough shot.
I just managed to stop the sun hitting the lens, without the shade appearing in
the image, or else the slide would have been filled with light flare.

Another view from Bardale Head, this time looking north down
Sleddale and towards the head of Wensleydale. The road often closes
here in winter, but farmers do a great job of shifting the snow away, and
I was able to scoot up just in my lowly Focus. The sheep were obviously
less perturbed by the cold than I was, but even they would be grateful
for the sun, which gives the psychological impression of warmth even
when it is freezing.

Sheep welcome the rising sun on the beautifully undulating
small hills near Bainbridge in Wensleydale.

Cowside Beck is one of my favourite features of the Dales. It cuts a huge scar across the landscape between the delightful Littondale and towards Malham Moor. I will be back again to try to find the perfect angle of the setting sun to hit the crags on the southern side, but here I used the vegetation near the road as a foreground to the final red light on the cliffs.

Two views of the magnificently well preserved Bolton Castle in Wensleydale. The first was snatched as quickly as possible, during a remarkable midge attack in July. Midges are here, and seem to be thriving! My guess would be to blame the recent cold winters. They are becoming a summer problem at various locations in the Dales. The second was in more relaxed circumstances, looking out to the south and the ever-present Penn Hill.

Pages 106–107 A rare collection of water in a land where most quickly drains or sinks into the porous limestone. Semer Water is tucked away, mostly out of sight of the main tourist alleyways, and is consequently a very tranquil and untroubled place. Here it is seen on a frosty morning In March, in remarkably clear light.

Early autumn 2012, and my final shot for this book which was effectively begun in 2004. I travelled to High Oxnop, between Swaledale and Wensleydale to see what autumn was idoing to the trees there. I found colour to be two weeks away, and light at the wrong angle for any satisfactory shots, but on descending I found an irresistible angle of Addlebrough near Askrigg. This book may be complete, but my work on the Dales will hopefully continue for many years, and I will find many more pleasant surprises.

PHOTOGRAPHER'S NOTE

My Yorkshire Dales project has effectively taken eight years from start to completion, although this hardly tells the full story, as there was quite a gap in the middle! I began shooting full panoramic images of Yorkshire in 2003, when I bought my first 617 film camera. Initially starting on the coast (leading to the publication of *The Yorkshire Coast* in 2006), I first shot in the Dales in 2004 beginning in Wensleydale, Swaledale and Ribblesdale, with a view to maybe a Yorkshire calendar or range of postcards. This ambition gradually expanded into a second Yorkshire book, on the Moors and Wolds in 2007, and a plan to complete the trilogy with the Dales shortly after.

Things didn't quite work out that way. I set off on various other projects, including a large book on the whole of England – great fun, but rather expensive on the petroleum – two books on London and one on Edinburgh. It wasn't until we moved to the very edge of the Dales near Bedale in 2010 that I fully resumed work on completing the trilogy. From here, access to Wensleydale is simple, and Swaledale and Nidderdale not much further. Driving to the south Dales can still take nearly 90 minutes (it's the second largest National Park of England), but it's hardly a chore.

I'm glad I took my time over the book. I think it has made for a much better volume than one that might have been released in a rush in 2007 or 2008. I was able to give my full attention to the subject and find locations I wasn't previous aware of. Plenty more to find too: I think our nomadic days are over now!

For the first time here I combine my traditional 617 film format with digital work.

I'd gone as far with film as I could. For a long time I thought I'd always use it, while it was still available. But then the price was much cheaper. I bought 2,000 rolls of 120 Velvia 50 once for £1 each, even saving an otherwise unemployed deep freeze to accomodate them. Now the cheapest I can manage is around £4.50 a roll. Given there's only four shots per roll with the 3:1 ratio 617, that works out at over £2 per shot once processing is added.

Finding a suitable digital option was always a big barrier. Here I must again give gratitude to Joe Cornish, who advised me that the first digital system he used, a Horseman SW-D, would be ideal for my style of photography. And so it has proved. The camera has a sliding back panel and the lens does not move to make panoramas, avoiding distortions and bending horizons. I simply take two shots with a Phase One digital back, on the left and right of the slider, and the resulting images match perfectly for stitching as they are from the same lens position. It's rather like having two halves of the same 617 film image and putting them back together. No trouble at all. It seems strange now how fearful I was of the digital conversion. The quality is very similar to 617 film. Some say better, some say worse: I will sit on the fence! At times the colours are rather different – the digital camera seems to saturate greens even more than Velvia 50 would – but there are ways and means of returning to a more natural look.

It's generally possible to tell which shots in the book are film and which are digital just from the size of the images. The film was always a strip of 3 x 1 ratio, while digital is fatter at 2.34 x 1. The width of my favourite lens for digital almost exactly matches that of film though, including the stitch, so if I prefer the 3 x 1 ratio I can always crop. There are one or two film images that have been cropped that might defy this rule, notably the Malham shot on pages 40–41.

The film cameras used were Fuji G617 (105mm lens), Fuji GX617 with 90mm, 105mm, 180mm and 300mm lenses, and my trusty Fotoman 617 with 180 and 300mm lenses. The film used here was always Velvia 50 asa, except for the picture on pages 4–5 of the train which moves far too fast for that! That one was on Provia 400x.

Lenses used on the Horseman body were 55mm and 90mm, quite closely matching the 105 and 180 film options. There is no real 300mm option for digital, so any shots requiring that telephoto lens will still be on film.

I still use the fantastic range of Lee filters, most commonly the ND hard graduated series, and 81 warm-up series. The Phase One digital seems to need as much warming as the cold blue Velvia film did, if not even more sometimes. Even now on digital from start to finish I want to get it right in camera. No high dynamic range techniques are used, and personally I would never use them for landscapes. Any photoshopping is about returning the photograph to the most natural look possible, removing colour casts that equipment or film scanning adds to the image.

The equipment is a form of barrier between my vision and the image. Fortunately what I use makes this a minor hurdle to overcome, to achieve more or less what I want.

Mark Denton, November 2012

ACKNOWLEDGMENTS

Mark Denton would like to thank Joe Cornish, Graham Merritt and Peter Sturt at Lee Filters, Arianna Osti and Andrew Dunn at Frances Lincoln, David Marshall, Richie 'Domestos Man' Dolan, and also many Dales locals for tips and suggestions.

Thank you to Rachel, Lucy and Sam for still putting up with him.

Prints from the book are available at www.markdentonphotographic.co.uk Mark also organises bespoke camera tuition in the Dales and beyond.

Enquiries can be addressed to markdentonphotographic@gmail.com

Setting up a 617 film camera for a vertical shot is tricky at the best of times, not least when standing in the flowing stream leading from Hardraw Force. But it was essential on this day. I'm not sure if I'll ever find better conditions here, as the strong autumnal sunshine bounced off the cliff and bathed the water in golden light.

INDEX

Aysgarth Falls has many sections and options for shooting, though I've generally found it a tricky place to get things right. This simple shot of the lower falls works here though. It's all about the exposure length here, to get the water movement just right. It turned out to be 2 seconds here. A low sun above helped light bounce of the surface and create a sculpted effect.